My
Blissful
Sun

Miguelina Ramirez

My Blissful Sun
Ramirez, Miguelina
miguelinaspoetry@gmail.com

ISBN 978-1-7389325-6-6 (Hardcover)
ISBN 978-1-7389325-7-3 (Paperback)
ISBN 978-1-7389325-8-0 (eBook)

Cover Design by Miguelina Ramirez
Edited by Katie Beaton , Veneration
Interior Design by Publish and Promote

The information is provided for entertainment and inspirational purposes only.

Contents

How does anyone's story start?
Mine starts with a rose, the moon, and the sun.
A little girl born in the Caribbean heat,
she longed for a cool breeze to fly her away
from uncertainty. A collection of poetry for
the little girl within me. I am proud of you.

Miguelina Ramirez

LIGHT

when I first saw you
I felt the sun's rays on my bare face
a warm and bright hue
dancing in colours of gold and white
this was the first time
I could see
with my eyes wide shut

POTENTIAL

if you could see yourself
the way I see you
then you'd know true beauty
a blossoming flower
with endless potential

YOURS

water lilies
beating sun
fascinated by your grace
wrap me in your glory
I want to know you
I want to hold you
I want to be yours

FAMILIAR

like your eyes
like your touch
like your voice
and the heat pressed between
the sheets at night

SALT

the way you taste
the way you feel on my cheeks
liberating and freeing
I release you with such ease

WHITE ROSES

as the heavens were created on the second day
you gifted me white roses
infused with our love
I watched them blossom
intertwine in each other's cultures
you looked deep into my eyes and whispered,
"La vida está mejor contigo,"
and I melted

PASTRIES & COFFEE

a euphoric, sugary bliss
a sweet tooth for you
for us
for this love
I crave

LEO

the essence of love
the essence of you
longing for hydration
you quench my thirst

Miguelina Ramirez

ORBIT

they say you create your reality
so did I create you?
a fragment of my imagination
you lie in the current version of myself
coexisting
specs of molecules floating in orbit
wanting to be touched
adored
held by someone who wasn't her past

LOVER

vintage blue jeans
oversized cardigan
you were my favourite memory
street lights and late-night talks
about me, about you, about us
to be 25

HUMAN

beating pulse
silent conversations held between
the fragments of our vibrations
you fill my life with such beauty
wisdom grows in quiet ways
lessons learned from day to day
I am only human

HANDS

like a moving train, we pass each other
hand in hand with other lovers
I saw your eyes
your faint smile disappeared
it hurt my ego
I wish you were near

TRAIN

on the midnight train with my lover
sleep in our eyes
you held on to me
with such force
I miss that force
even if it was just for a moment

ART

art makes you feel
like a breath caught in time,
when all of your senses align
a fleeting spark in the heat of the moment
time stops, and your mind begins to wander

CANVAS

thick strokes of colour
I am your muse
running your fingertips across my canvas
rich, deep in red and gold
in oil's natural glow
secrets will show
we create art

CHURCH

a museum full of art, what a beauty
my eyes indulge in Rome's history, culture
and food—a soulful language
that brings millions together
the art of self-expression
the art of love
the art of being still

Miguelina Ramirez

THE ONE

when you have found the one
it's a gentle knowing, a silent peace
in the midst of a crowded room
his gaze will stay
and chase doubt away

FLORENCE

a fiery kiss, a golden halo
hues of bliss coat the skyline
a beauty much felt, rather than seen
a tender shade, a claiming scene

LONDON

a soul that longs for adventure
experiencing life and its beauty
you inspire me
our souls in tune
I met you in the south

MOMENT

art, like the sun setting in mid-July
or your hair brushed against my chest
I ponder the moment
we first met

US

you and me
on a boat in the Mediterranean Sea
loving life, loving us
holding on to nothing
but each other

LEARN

can I learn to love you?
the way you love me
the way you hold me
the way you kiss me
searching for fault in your eyes
yet I only see my reflection
am I the common denominator?

Miguelina Ramirez

LIGHTHOUSE

a ripping current, I am your wave
drown your sorrows in my bay
I will be your lighthouse

LIFE VEST

you showed me the world
when there was nothing left to see
you showed me your tears
when I was numb and still
filled my scars with kisses
weathered my storms
through rain and thunder
you were a steady hand
a constant view
my life vest
pure and true
you stayed with me

Miguelina Ramirez

MOON

the moon river stood still,
a calming storm, you washed up on the shore
sand pressed between your toes,
a spark in your eyes
I could no longer resist you

LUNA

I have watched many sunsets
but nothing compares to the one standing in
front of me
your soulful beauty sinks battleships
my darling

GAZE

baby blue
like the ocean
like the sky
like your eyes
staring back at me

OCEAN

mighty and deep
an endless blue
full of mysteries and wonders
where waves crash into stillness
and stillness crashes into night

Miguelina Ramirez

BODY OF WATER

drifting away, I hear the waves crash
I love the way the ocean hugs my curves
hugs my heart
here, I am enough

SAILBOAT

crashing waves connected by
the mighty ocean
I see the beauty in life
and life sees the beauty in me

REFLECTION

gratitude for life
gratitude for you
I trust in the divine planning
of a single soul
becoming two

SKY

I am the day
you are the night
and that's okay

Miguelina Ramirez

SHADOWS

they say that light and darkness cannot mix
where shadows become dusk and daylight fades
a dance between tones
two worlds intertwining as lovers
held in a balance

BALANCE

I deserve to be loved
the way I love others

Miguelina Ramirez

LESSONS

you are my favourite mistake
even when the lessons tend to fade
when they hurt too much
they numb the pain

UNDEFEATED

it may feel like the end
but darling, it's just the beginning
put one foot forward
water your seeds
and watch them blossom

Miguelina Ramirez

ENERGY

what you are seeking
is seeking you
energies align
I am your vibration

HEALING

a bridge between souls
like the full moon pulling the tides
emotions are pulled to the surface
align with nature's vibration
my eyes won't open all the way
as I have been expecting this shift
the inner healing starts today

WRITER

directing a play
where you play all roles
the script might change
but you will always be the writer

DAYDREAM

lessons not yet learned
we departed ways
downtown bars
midnight kisses
slow dances to our song
you held my hips
with such ease
until I woke up
from this dream

Miguelina Ramirez

2 A.M.

the world is silent
but my thoughts are not

TV

visions forming in colour
you are static electricity
passing through my mind
you kiss me
one last time

LUST

you could be the best thing for me
but do I want to get better?
I love it when you call my name
I love it when you stutter
set me free and be on your way
for this love is not mutual

DIALOGUE

tinted windows
but the sunlight still gets through
just like my thoughts for you
I want to stand in your presence
but in my mind, you don't speak
our love has ended
though it feels strange and bleak
I do hope one day
we may speak

PAGES

finding peace with who I am
the shining light inside of me
embracing every scar
expressing my emotions with a pen and paper
as you read my pages
a work of art
the body tells a story
and your eyes listen

BUTTERFLIES

water droplets may break my wings
but I have learned to rest
during the storms of life
beneath its depths, a world unknown
I choose to live in any storm

Miguelina Ramirez

STORM

I find comfort in the thunder
rain droplets pressed against the windowsill
empathy lingers in my thoughts
I must give myself grace
for the things I cannot control

RAIN

I love the sound of rain
washing away the dust and stains
retaining the earth's warm embrace
I find peace in this rebirth

POWER OF DANCE

I allow this church to move through me
like a choir singing from the heavens
I surrender to this feeling
miles of resentment dissipate with the shake of
my hips
what once was held, and felt
is set aside
with open palms, my soul unwinds
the beauty in letting go
a sweet release
I now find my peace

STARRY NIGHT

you were stargazing at the heavens
I was stargazing at you
beneath the velvet sky
vast and so deep
a distant song formed in my chest
your eyes lost in the stars
my lips lost in your grace

AUTUMN

lost in the mountains, just you and me
in the quiet of the night where no one goes
hand in hand with my lover
tracing paths that touch the sky
I heard the whispering of the pines
"you are almost free."

WILLOW TREE

in roots and branches, the soul exists
a sweeping view of nature's embrace
a crispy autumn breeze sways the willow tree
with roots embedded in the earth
there's a claiming grace
to the way life plays
a mighty role in our lives

Miguelina Ramirez

THE HIKE

hiking trails and nature air
cures an overthinking mind
and in the climb, echoes reflect
I find my peace, heart, and breath

LUNGS

you are the rush of wind
that my lungs so desperately need
a fresh breeze loving every inch of me
you are my inhaler
and inhale, I do

BIRDS

how do you fly so high
soaring in the wind
without a care in the world?
I have always felt a special connection
to these feathered friends

TRUE NORTH

and even though I no longer live up north
a working town full of oil and gas
long working hours
shifts made to last
this small town taught me
how to spread my wings to the south
grateful for the life lessons
and the many blessings

Miguelina Ramirez

BODY

the seasons are changing
and I'm getting older
as time moves onward
my skin's barrier forms lines
like a map of where I've been
wrinkles bloom where memories live
in gentle lines
traces of a life well spent

LET GO

the art of letting go:
people, places
and things that no longer serve you
release and protect your peace

SNOW

winter frost, a silver lace
a fragile beauty, a cold embrace
transforms into a blanket of white overnight
though soft and chilly to the touch
a snowflake's beauty is unmatched
thankful for the season

LOCKDOWN

no words, just silence
a deep stillness, a quiet thread
and these stolen moments
in the eyes of today's youth

END

and in the end, when we are old and grey
nothing else will matter
but the memories we cherished
with the people who loved us
life is indeed magical

SEASONS

violet summers
crispy winters,
you're aging well
head out of the window
a carefree summer teen
jamming to '90s music
you have a lust for life

MAX

throwing a football brings you joy
the field is set, and the whistle blows
green grass and a cheering crowd
their mighty screams heard for miles
a rhythm beats within your chest
for the love of football
you make us proud

PAPER PLANES

paper planes, fly me away, with your dip and dive
and gentle toss, tracing dreams in social studies
my wandering mind
young and innocent
I miss my Caribbean mother

Miguelina Ramirez

FOREST

lush greenery, a wide forest
full of life and wonder
you house many spirits
old and young
the trees tell stories
Costa Rica in all its glory

A MOM'S LOVE

it was like coming home for Christmas
when you haven't seen your family in a while
unconditional devotion
words unspoken and full of grace
no conditions and no blame
unmoved by time
just in stillness
I love you, Mother
to pieces

Miguelina Ramirez

PEI

rich in soil and deep oceans
Prince Edward Island is home for me
surrounded by family, my heart's content
the island canvas is vast and grand
painted by an unseen hand
this is nature's beautiful land

NATURE

nothing compares to the beauty nature shares
law and order stretch for miles
where flowers bloom and creatures thrive
I am one with the earth
where the sun dips low
and the ocean meets
in perfect harmony

COMFORT

the way you look at me
the way you admire me
the way you rub your head across the pillow
the way you unconditionally love me for me
even without the kitty treats
with your earthy vibrations
humming a beat
you are my comfort

FAITH

faith moves mountains
just wait and see
it guides us through the day and night
with some curiosity
strong and hopeful
in my faith in love
for it brings the world together

LOVE

love is medicine
for the young and the old
for the lost and the broken
love wins wars

SOFT

a soft life, free of life's stresses
free of toxic exes
a life full of love, smiles, and midnight dances
a life full of you

BABY

a wedding dress
a veil
your touch
my laugh
our story now begins

PURITY

running barefoot
with open arms
through a field of grass
with my sweet love
sunlight coating our smiling faces
in this moment
we are pieces of the sun

www.ingramcontent.com/pod-product-compliance
Lightning Source LLC
Chambersburg PA
CBHW071109090426
42737CB00013B/2545